Effective Parenting

by
James B. Stenson

*All booklets are published thanks to the
generous support of the members of the
Catholic Truth Society*

CATHOLIC TRUTH SOCIETY

PUBLISHERS TO THE HOLY SEE

Contents

All rights reserved. First published 2013 by The Incorporated Catholic Truth Society, 40-46 Harleyford Road London SE11 5AY Tel: 020 7640 0042 Fax: 020 7640 0046. This edition © 2013 The Incorporated Catholic Truth Society. The book is printed with permission of Scepter Publishers, New Rochelle, NY. No reproduction of any kind is permitted without permission of the Catholic Truth Society

ISBN 978 1 86082 866 9

A Job Description for Parents?

"I wish I had known all this 25 years ago!" That's what I've sometimes been told after my conferences on successful parent leadership. The words, said in humour but sometimes with wistful regret, came from older parents whose children had already grown and left home.

I have written on parent leadership, the fruit of my 30 years' experience with families, so that you, a young parent, won't have to express this same regret in the future. I've written this booklet so that you can form a clearer idea of how other parents have lived as great leaders in family life and have succeeded with their sacred mission: to raise their children right. I want to help you form a 'job description', so to speak, on how to succeed as a leader to your children.

When I say 'succeed or fail', I don't mean parents' methods of discipline, or how they keep their children under control, or how they handle the daily challenges in family life. These are short-term achievements, but only part of the whole picture.

Parents really win success with their children only in the long term. Parents succeed with their children when they grow up to become competent, responsible, considerate and generous men and women who are committed to live by principles of integrity - adults who bring honour to their parents all their lives through their conduct, conscience and character. Raising children to become adults like this is what parenthood is all about.

In my experience, busy parents today need to think carefully about what they're doing to raise their children well, that is, to become men and women of conscience and character. After all, parents have one chance - and only one - to raise their children.

What I set out for you in this booklet is intended to be descriptive, not prescriptive. That is, I don't claim to have all the answers about family life, and I don't know anyone who does. What I'm doing here is describing the kind of thinking and action - the compass of parenthood - that great parents have lived by and taught me in the course of my professional career. If you find something here of help to you, then this booklet has done its job.

James Stenson
Easter 2013

The Vision of Parent Leaders

Any time people engage in an important, responsible undertaking for another's welfare - whether a business, job, government matter or a family - there is a need for clear, competent leadership. The more serious the challenge, the greater the need for someone to direct everyone's efforts in an inspiring, encouraging way towards the ultimate goal. To this end, the real mission for parents is to raise their children towards responsible adulthood. All the dynamics of family life lead to the question of what kind of men and women the children will grow to be. No challenge is more important than this, and so great parents emerge in family life as real leaders.

How do fathers and mothers lead their children effectively? To form a picture of parental leadership, let us look at the characteristics of leaders and see how parents fit the profile of leadership in family life.

Having vision

Leaders are moved by a distant vision, and they thus win people's respect. A broad statement that you will probably agree with is that in business and professional life, and in affairs of state, our most respected leaders are those who look farthest toward the future and foresee oncoming perils and opportunities. Respected leadership and strategic foresight go hand in hand. The farther and clearer the vision, the greater the respect. It seems that this dynamic works in successful families, too. Parents - all kinds with different temperaments - succeed in family life through their confident leadership.

The confidence of mission

Successful parents base their confidence in knowing they have this sacred mission to carry out with their children. They see themselves *raising adults, not children*. They have been called by God to carry out a job, and that holy task is this: to lead their children - with daily sacrificial effort - to grow into confident, responsible, considerate, generous men and women who are committed to live by Christian principles all their lives, no matter what the cost. Being conscious of this mysterious and sacred mission, holding it always before their eyes, is what turns these parents into great men and women themselves, real heroes to their children, and makes their family life together a great, rollicking, beautiful adventure.

Setting the bar high

Effective parent leaders look at their children and picture them 20 years from now, as grown men and women with job and family responsibilities of their own. They seem to understand a truth of life: children will tend to grow up to our expectations or down to them. So, these parent leaders set high ideals for their children's later lives. They think of their children's future along these lines:

- The children will have excellent judgement, especially in the choice of a spouse and the upbringing of their own children.

- They will centre their lives in a stable, permanent, happy marriage - raising a great family like the one they grew up in.

- They will succeed in their careers, whatever these may be - doing work they enjoy, pitching their powers against problems for the welfare of others.

- They will be able to support their families comfortably, but not luxuriously, for a life of excess, they know, may destroy their children (the parents' grandchildren).

- They will be generous to friends and those in need.

- They will never live as quitters, slackers, whiners or cowards - nor will they let their own children live this way.

- They will be nobody's fool or pushover. They will not be swayed by charlatans. They will know nonsense when they see it.

- When they have erred, they will face the truth and apologise. They will not let their pride stand in the way of truth and justice, especially in family life.

- They will be esteemed by all who know them for their honesty, integrity, hard work, generosity, religious commitment and good humour.

- They will remain close to their brothers and sisters for life, giving and receiving encouragement and support.

- They will live by their parents' principles. They will have a conscience for life - the voice of their parents' lessons of right and wrong - and they will pass these lessons on to their own children.

- Their whole lives will be moved by love - the willingness to endure and overcome anything for the welfare and happiness of others, starting with their family.

Learning to act

Consider this: public monuments are never set up to honour someone who *intended* to do something. Leaders act. Though they spend time in study and planning, they mostly act. For leaders, study and planning are a ramp-up for action, not a substitute for it. Moreover, real leaders never let indecision lead to inaction. When confronted with several tough choices of action, they do not shrink back. They brace themselves, choose what they judge as the best way forward, and then set to work as best they can.

Sometimes great leadership means just this: doing the best you can with what you have. If you are climbing a mountain, you sometimes have to backtrack or surmount obstacles or thrash your way through tangled shortcuts - but as long as you keep moving upward, you will reach the summit. The one thing you do not do is quit. Neglect - to do nothing - is the worst mistake of all.

Foresight

Parent leaders, too, understand the consequences of neglect. They know they have a job to do - a change to effect - in the minds and hearts of their growing children. And they draw courage to act from foreseeing what awful things could happen to their children if that job remains undone, if their children retain the flaws and selfishness of childhood into adult life. For instance: if our children remain self-centred - 'Me first!' - they will neglect or mistreat others, and their marriages and careers will fly apart.

- If they have no conscience, they will have no inner strength to resist temptation. They could cave in easily to peer-pressure and meet with disasters: drugs, alcohol abuse, recreational sex, trouble with the law.

- If they never learn to say 'please' and 'thank you' on their own, without prompting, they will remain as self-centred people with little sense of gratitude.

- If they do not respect their parents' authority, they will have trouble with all other rightful authority: teachers, employers, the law, God himself.

- If they receive no life-directing guidance from their parents in childhood, they may desperately need guidance later from parent-substitutes: marriage counsellors, physicians or mental-health professionals.

- If they form no principled framework for assessing people's character, they may marry people who will not love them as they deserve.

- If they cannot manage their own affairs, they will find it difficult to take care of others.

- If they do not keep their promises, they cannot keep commitments - not to spouse, nor children, nor employers.

- If they never learn to set and meet goals, they cannot set and meet ideals.

- If they form a habit of lying, they will not be considered trustworthy.

- If they never learn to balance healthy work and play, their lives could shuttle between drudgery and debauchery. If they never learn to be confident producers, they will live as lifelong adolescent consumers.

- If they remain lazy and sloppy in work, they will be shoved aside by their competition.

- If they see work as 'hassle' to be shunned, they will have wobbly, precarious careers - or will see work as adolescents see it: purely a source of money.

- If they always expect to have their way, their adult lives will be ravaged by anger and frustration because they will not have learned to bear disappointment.

- If they sulk and bear grudges, they will muddle through life as smouldering, self-pitying victims - and never amount to anything.

- If they remain as egocentric children, they may shun having children of their own.

- As the saying goes, those who do not stand for something will fall for anything.

Rules That Make a Family Work

The word 'we' is a powerful force in family life. It is what anchors children's loyalty to their parents and siblings - and forges a lifelong bond to their parents' convictions of right and wrong. It empowers children's inner voice of conscience for life.

The importance of family loyalty

Family loyalty saves many teenagers and young adults from disaster. Well-raised young people will shun drugs, drunkenness and other reckless behaviour, not only because these are wrong, but because, if caught, the teenagers would disgrace their family. Fear of causing their family shame can steel the will of young people, lead them to shrug off peer pressures, say 'no' to selfish impulses and live rightly.

How does this loyalty come about? Through the power of 'we....'

The importance of family rules

Every healthy family lives by a set of rules in the home, some high standards for attitudes and conduct directed toward the welfare of others. When children live by these standards every day for years, they gradually - with stops and starts along the way - internalise powers of judgement, ethical responsibility, perseverance and consideration for others. Active family rules form the framework for their growth in character.

Why does a healthy family have to have rules? For one reason: because it has a *job* to do, a *service mission* to carry out. A consumerist family, by contrast, has no job at all - for consumption is a static pastime, not an achievement - and so it has no reason to lay down standards for performance.

If we look at the parental job from a professional point of view - that is, the way things work in any serious business enterprise whether a business, a non-profit service, a society and its government, or a family - we see three basic elements that distinguish it from a loose and pointless or amateurish operation:

1. **A *mission*.** This is some long-term goal of service, a task carried out for the betterment of others.

2. **A *responsible chain of command*.** In any group, some people assume the burden of responsibility and consequently hold the authority to lead; they teach and direct others to carry out the institution's mission and deliver its service. In this way, responsible leaders direct those who work with them, not just under them - for, as we've seen before, a real leader has joiners, not followers.

3. A *set of performance standards*. These are clear directional rules by which those in charge show others what is expected of them, the ways they most effectively contribute to the overall mission. In business this includes a job description and some sort of protocol that sets standards for acceptable performance (office rules, by-laws, contractual obligations and the like).

Because every healthy family is a serious service enterprise, it displays all three elements outlined here: mission, leadership and performance standards. On the other hand, since the consumerist family is going nowhere - having no real directed mission - then the parents are weak leaders (lead where?) and the family's rules, if any, act only as ad hoc bandages to keep hassles and damage to a minimum.

The duty of parents

Obviously a father and mother take on a serious mission in family life. Since they assume this huge responsibility, mum and dad have the right and duty to lead. All children need leadership, and if both parents do not lead them to do right, then someone else may lead them to do wrong.

In my many conversations with great parents and their children, I used to probe from time to time to learn what rules each healthy family lived by. I noticed two key points. First, there is a sense of positive teamwork:ll the rules, directly or implicitly, began with the word 'We...,' not 'you...'

For instance, the rule for chores was not "*You children must clean your room,*" but rather "*We all pitch in to keep this house in decent shape.*" Not "*You must call if you're late,*" but instead "*We call if we're going to be late.*" It wasn't "*You have to put toys away,*" but "*We all return things where they belong.*"

In other words, *the parents lived by the rules themselves, the same ones they imposed on their children.* The parents lived at home like responsible, considerate adults, and they insisted their children do the same. Like any other real leaders, mum and dad demanded as much of themselves as of their children. They practised what they preached and led the way by their personal example. Consequently, every day, their children witnessed the parents' convictions alive in ongoing action. (And so, later as teenagers, they could never justly accuse their parents of hypocrisy.) Second, there is encouragement of virtue:

Abiding by these rules led the children - or forced them - to practise each of the virtues. Repeatedly, every day, mum and dad encouraged their children to live rightly: to take responsibility, manage their own affairs, work conscientiously, discern right from wrong, respect their parents' authority and consider the needs and rights of others. Right living permeated the whole spirit of the family - and seeped its way inside the children little by little, day by day. An old maxim says, "As the day goes, so goes one's life." Whatever the children practise every day - for good or for ill - will be the way they live later.

In a sense, the dynamic by which children learned the virtues through these rules seemed to follow the wise adage: what children *hear*, they mostly forget. What they *see*, they mostly remember. What they *do*, they understand and internalise.

All the rules seemed to fall into five distinct but interconnected categories:

Respecting the rights and sensibilities of others

Examples under this heading might include saying 'please,' 'thank you,' 'I'm sorry,' 'I give my word of honour' as appropriate; not being rude to others; not telling tales, swearing, making disparaging remarks, gossiping or otherwise criticising others (though if someone we know is, for example, dabbling in drugs, then for their sake we report it to whoever can help in time); respecting the privacy of family affairs; telling the truth; not arguing when corrected; only making promises we can keep; respecting other's property; showing special respect to older people; celebrating each other's accomplishments.

Contributing equally to making the home a pleasant place to inhabit

Examples under this heading might include cleaning up after ourselves immediately; not bringing outdoor activities indoors (no ball-playing, running and chasing, missile throwing, wrestling or excessive shouting); closing doors quietly; not shouting messages to people in other rooms; only eating in designated areas (kitchen, dining room); returning borrowed items promptly; carrying out all our chores to the best of our ability; not aiming for 'results' as such, but rather for personal best effort.

Communicating appropriately

Examples include gaining prior permission - with, say, at least a day's notice - for important and potentially disruptive activities (sleepovers and the like); returning from social events at a reasonable hour, one previously agreed upon; in general, working to avoid unpleasant surprises and unnecessary worry in the family.

*Only using electronic media and games
to promote family welfare*

Examples include using television and other gadgets sparingly and with discernment; making most recreation non-electronic (reading, games, hobbies, sports or conversation); permitting nothing in the home that offends moral principles and/or treats other people as objects (no pornography, which objectifies women, no racist, sexist or ethnic disparagement etc); keeping noise to a reasonable level so as not to disturb others.

Loving and honouring our creator above all things; thanking him for his blessings and asking his help for our needs and those of others.

Examples might include thanking the Lord by worshipping him together as a family; striving to live by his commandments of right and wrong; respecting the conscience and rights of others who worship him differently; praying especially before meals and bedtime; living in the confidence that God watches over us with his loving fatherly protection; knowing that God commands all of us to honour our father and mother, and that the finest way we do this is to adopt our parents' values, live by them all our lives, and pass them on to our own children whole and intact.

It's your call

There you have them, the rules most commonly found in great families. For whatever use they may be to you, they have been listed here; but once again let me stress that what is laid out above is *de*scriptive, not *pre*scriptive. That is, I am describing what I have seen work in one great family after another. I do not presume to dogmatise about details here, or insist that every family should adopt these standards wholesale. I could not rightly do that even if I wanted to.

Let me stress, too, that practically no family lives by each and every one of these rules. I have simply listed all of them here for your thoughtful judgement. It is up to you to weigh each one and judge what is best for you and your children. It is your family, and therefore your call.

To live by them perfectly every day is, of course, an impossible ideal. For both parents and children, some backsliding and flawed performance is absolutely normal. All the same, these rules are fixed in place as what we try to live by, a 'resting place' for our conscience - like the home keys on a piano or computer keyboard to which our fingers always return. The people in a great family never attain perfection, but they never stop trying. To keep trying, no matter what, is the essence of greatness.

Discipline in the Family

The word 'discipline' has had a bad press. It's widely misunderstood to mean punishment. But it does not mean punishment. Nor does it mean control for its own sake. And it does not mean enforcing rules just for the sake of minimising hassles at home, a kind of damage control.

Understanding discipline

Discipline certainly involves occasional punishment and some control, as well as clear guidelines for behaviour. But its real meaning is far deeper and more important. Discipline really means confident, effective leadership.

Look at it this way. The word 'discipline' is related to the word 'disciple,' and it springs from the Latin word meaning 'to learn.' Discipline is what happens when some leader teaches and his disciples learn. Broadly speaking, discipline means teaching and learning, leading and joining.

Discipline and the family

To repeat the key idea here, discipline in family life means teaching the children to acquire - by personal example, directed practice and verbal explanation (in that order) - the great virtues of sound judgement, a sense of responsibility, personal courage, self-control and magnanimity. These take root in the give and take of family life and then flower to healthy maturity through the steady nourishment of confident, unified parental leadership. All this takes years.

So, discipline (that is, teaching) requires planning and patience as much as occasional swift corrective action. It calls for example-giving as much as rules, and encouragement and praise as much as loving denial and just punishment. It means living in the family such that children are made to do what is right - as the parents see this - and shun what is wrong, and to explain the differences so compellingly that the children will remember the lessons all their lives and then pass them on to their children. That is the long and the short of it: discipline in the family is moral leadership, starting from the parents.

True discipline starts with parental authority

Let us start with an absolutely basic principle: your rights of authority in the family.

Effective parent leaders understand that parenthood is not an elective office; you do not have to curry favour with your children. Your rights as a parent come with the job, with your responsibility. In the home as in business, authority and responsibility - rights and duties - must go hand in hand; you cannot have one without the other. The two have to be proportional, of equal heft. If you were handed a tough assignment at work, but were denied the power and resources to carry it out, you would be stuck with the burden of your duties, and no doubt seethe with resentment at this injustice. Nobody - in any human situation - can bear responsibility without the power to carry it out.

The truth about parental responsibility

As a parent, you take on enormous responsibility. You are responsible for your children's welfare, and for this you answer to the law, to society, to your conscience, to your creator. In fact - and this is something parents seldom think about - you will even answer later to your grown children; someday they will look back and judge you, up or down, for the way you dealt with them in childhood.

So when a man and woman become parents, they take on rights as well. They confidently claim the authority - the power to choose and decide - that they must possess to lead their children responsibly, to keep them from harm.

Authority means, among other things, the right to be obeyed. Smart parents may harbour quiet doubts about many things in family life, but they never doubt their right to their children's obedience. They assert this right, as they assert all their other rights, in a clear, no-nonsense way. But they do this with understanding and affection: they are 'affectionately assertive,' and this is the essence of parental leadership.

Affectionate assertiveness

All the effective parents I have known practise what might be called *affectionate assertiveness*. That is, they *assert* correct conduct and attitudes by their example, action and words. At the same time they are unfailingly affectionate with their children. They correct their children because they love them, want to protect them, and care above all else for their future welfare and happiness.

They set out to *correct the fault, not the person*. They 'hate the sin, love the sinner.' They are willing, on occasion, to risk being temporarily unpopular with a wayward son or daughter - knowing that their future happiness is at stake, and that their children will someday thank them and revere them as great parents.

Showing affection

How do you show affection to your children?

Make physical contact

You welcome them on your knee and embrace them. You take their hand while walking together. You playfully squeeze them on the shoulder or arm. When walking by them as they are seated, you pat them on the head or ruffle their hair. You invite them to sit next to you and pat them when they sit down. You give them a wink and a smile. You tell corny jokes and laugh at theirs. You tell funny stories and find other ways to share a good laugh, without offending anyone. You whisper sweet things in their ears. (Sometimes, when you feel like shouting something at your small children, have them sit on your lap instead and whisper it into their ear; this never fails to get their attention. And your correction comes across affectionately, as it should.)

Show happiness and pride in their accomplishments

You make praise every bit as specific as blame. (Parents tend to make blame specific, but to put praise in vague generalities: "You've been a good girl this morning...") Praise them for a job well done, even when they have done it as punishment or as an obligation: "You did a great job making your bed this morning..." "Your room is spick and span, just the way it should be..." "Your homework looks neat and professional, and I am proud of you...." Children need sincere praise from time to time. In fact, we all do. One of people's greatest needs, at any age, is sincere appreciation.

Talk with them

When you tuck them into bed, linger for a bit, just a couple of minutes, to make small talk. Bedtime is a great occasion to talk things over with children, and listen to them. All their lives, they will fondly remember their bedtime chats with mum and dad.

You can talk with them while driving, doing dishes and other chores together, walking and biking, working on hobbies you share, tucking them into bed. If you cut down on television watching or computer time, you will find slivers and chunks of time here and there. Make the time, and never forget you haven't much of it left - your children will grow up with incredible swiftness.

Look at them with affection

With both sons and daughters, show affection with your eyes; as well as with your ears, listen to your children with your eyes. Look at them with love. When you deliberately make eye contact with them, especially when they are speaking to you, you show how much you care for them. In your eyes they can read your soul - your love for them, your pride in them, your hopes for their future.

Correct with love

Somehow, mysteriously, normal children sense when their parents correct them out of love. Great parents correct *because* they love. Even though children dislike the correction itself, deep down they grasp the love behind their parents' direction. Sooner or later as they grow up, they understand that their parents' occasional wrath is aimed at their faults, not them personally.

Since you, as a parent, show plenty of affection in normal, non-confrontational situations in family life (which is most of the time), and because you always show willingness to forgive once apologies are made and punishment completed, your children sense the truth - that your whole life, including episodes of corrective punishment, devotes itself to their happiness. Later, as young adults, and even before they're out of their teens, they will fully understand why your love moved you to act as you did, and they will thank you.

Ways to correct misbehaviour

So, these things being said, what can you do to punish misbehaviour in fairly serious matters? Here is a list drawn from parents' experience for younger children; please see the later chapter for advice with teenagers:

Be physical and firm, but not violent

Physically, but painlessly, restrain the children. Take them by the hand or arm and remove them to someplace private. Take both hands in yours, hold the children still, and look them in the eye. Say what you have to say in a low but "I-mean-business" way and keep at it until they've understood and said they are sorry.

Remove them physically and make them spend what some parents call 'time out' - a few minutes of isolation away from the family, even in a closed room. Don't let them return until they've said they're sorry. (For very young children, you may have to supervise their time in a corner or some other 'punishment spot.')

For older children, remove privileges. This means no games or television or use of the telephone.

Give them helpful work to do

Put them to work. Have a so-called 'job jar' at home. This is a receptacle containing slips of paper describing jobs to be done around the house. Let the malefactor pick out three slips and then choose one, which must then be done to your satisfaction. Also, if children complain they're 'bored' around the house, direct them to the job jar. Parents who do this hardly ever hear complaints from their children about boredom. The word 'boring' disappears from the family vocabulary.

Get them to work together

If two siblings are quarrelling and won't stop after one warning, put both of them to work on the same project: cleaning dishes, raking leaves, gardening, washing the car. This treatment usually brings about a reconciliation.

I have to insert a parenthesis here: for many children, being banished to the bedroom is scarcely a punishment at all. Children's rooms can be an Aladdin's cave of stereos, radio, television and electronic games galore. Their rooms are essentially entertainment centres surrounding a bed.

From what I can see, many healthy families hold firmly to this policy: each child's bedroom is a place for study, reading and sleep - full stop. Entertainment gadgets are only for common areas of the house, where people can enjoy them together. This policy has the happy side effect of eliminating distractions from homework. It works. And the children learn a truth about life: when we try to work and play at the same time, we end up doing neither - leisure is really enjoyable only when we've earned it.

Look forward!

In any event, whatever method of correction you use and whatever ways of cultivating discipline you carry out within your family, see it as an investment that will later yield high return. Once you've established your authority in their youngest years, then you've won most of the battle. When they're older, just a businesslike warning or flashing-eyed glare from you, or even your expression of 'disappointment', usually works to restore cooperation. By that time, the children know you mean business.

Parental teamwork

Parents who live this affectionate assertiveness work with each other to plan out different lessons of responsibility (that is, punishments) in response to their children's varying types of misbehaviour. This is important. The more carefully these responses are thought out beforehand and thus made routine in family life, the calmer and more consistent both parents can be in handling their childrens' provocations.

This rational structure avoids, or at least minimises, the problem in many ineffective families, especially when dealing with teenagers - impromptu punishments imposed in anger, often harsh and overreactive, and resented as unfair.

Remember, you can be tough with normal children and quite effective with them if, and only if, they perceive that you're trying to be fair.

Correcting effectively

Here is a rational structure for imposing memorable correction on the children for their wayward ways. It's based on a sound principle from military history: Those generals who chose their battlegrounds ahead of time usually managed to win - Hannibal at Cannae, Wellington at Waterloo, Lee at Fredericksburg, Eisenhower at Normandy.

Choose your battleground. Don't scatter your resources trying to correct the children every single time they do wrong. If you tried this, you'd soon need to be fitted for a straitjacket.

Instead, establish three levels of misbehaviour, each calling for proportionately heavy response. In rising order of seriousness, these could be thought of in the following terms:

Misdemeanours

These are minor infractions, just childish misdeeds arising from inexperience, thoughtlessness, reckless impulsiveness - such as tracking mud in the house, noisy brawling, throwing missiles indoors, forgetting (that is, honestly forgetting) to do chores, failing to put things away. A lot of these habits will be outgrown anyway.

These misdeeds call for quick but low-level response, or sometimes just letting the matter go. It's like the quality control system in a factory: try to catch a sample every few times. You don't need to correct minor goofs every single time, and you might go crazy if you tried.

Serious infractions

These are acts where children infringe on the rights of others, especially siblings - causing offense by name-calling, taking property without permission, physical aggression, refusing to give or accept apology, using profanity and similar deeds of more serious injustice. Though you can occasionally overlook the misdemeanours mentioned above, you *must* correct these serious lapses of justice and charity practically every single time.

Never forget, every time you correct your children's injustices, their infringements on the rights of others, you are forming their lifelong conscience and ethics. You are preparing them for the way they will later treat their spouses, children and professional colleagues. So there is a lot at stake here. Don't let up and don't give up.

Felony infractions

These are serious matters that endanger your children's welfare, either now or later in life, and they call for the severest punishment every single time, whatever this might be.

For the youngest children this category obviously includes whatever physically endangers them now: playing with fire, wandering into the street, poking metal objects into electrical outlets and the like. Punishment should be swift and memorable. It seems that nearly all parents, even the most pacifist, react this way instinctively.

But equally important are those wrongdoings that threaten children's welfare later on as adults - those acts that imperil their basic concepts of respect for rightful authority and the importance of personal integrity. You must impose swift, serious punishment every time your children do the following:

- Show disrespect for you personally - call you names, try to strike you, raise their voice in anger at you, say that they 'hate' you.

- Attempt to defy your authority - for example, saying 'no' or otherwise refusing to comply with your direction, or deliberately 'forgetting' to do so. This pertains even in relatively minor matters, especially after you've given warning. If you direct your child to clean up a mess of his and he refuses or just walks away, then the issue becomes one of authority, not just clean-up. You must not permit him to get away with this defiance.

- Deliberately lie to you, especially after being put on their honour to tell the truth.

These three areas are vitally important for your children's welfare. Everything you have to teach your children depends on their respect for you and for your authority and for their own word of honour. If you lose this, you lose them.

As a last pointer, don't shout at your children all the time. It's a waste of breath. If one of your children needs a talking to, take him or her out for a walk or sit down and have a drink - and say what you have to say in a calm, serious way. Don't forget to listen, either - for your childrens' view of things, though wrong, may still have a point. A couple of heart-to-heart talks are better than a dozen explosions.

Considering your children's rights

Effective parents combine rightful authority with respect for their children's rights. Children do have rights, of course. Not because they're children, but because they are people; and all people, even young ones, have certain basic rights. Here are the rights that great parents keep in mind as they exercise moral leadership in the family:

Right to privacy (up to a point)

Children need a certain security of privacy. For instance, they should have a place of their own to keep personal effects away from prying by other family members. And their normal, above-board dealings with friends should be respected as personal, essentially no one's business but theirs.

Naturally, these privacy rights are not absolute, just as they're not absolute in adult society either. Sometimes privacy rights must give way before higher necessity; for instance, the law can force testimony under oath about some personal affairs, and it makes allowances for 'reasonable search' in criminal investigations. So, too, in your family. Your children's privacy rights give way to your parental rights wherever some serious danger suggests itself - for instance, in possible involvement with drugs, or what you perceive as excessive intimacy with the opposite sex.

In normal circumstances, *parents who respect their children's privacy generally find that their children grow to be open and sincere with them*. If you respect their rights, they will respect your judgement, and then come to you with the truth. It is control-oriented, excessively prying parents who find their children close-mouthed, secretive and sneaky.

Right to presumption of innocence

Don't rush to judgement. Listen to your children's side of things, especially in dealing with your older children, and most especially when you did not personally witness the alleged misdeed. But by the same token, never undercut your spouse if it was he or she who witnessed things. If you think your spouse is mistaken or overreactive, then discuss the matter privately.

Right not to be publicly embarrassed

Whenever you can, make corrections personally and privately, as you would in business. If you bawl at your child in front of siblings or friends, the lesson is probably lost. Your child's resentment at public humiliation acts like static to cancel out your message. Corrections made privately - eyeball to eyeball - go straight to the point.

Right to just punishment

An angry, overreactive punishment easily skyrockets way out of proportion to the original provocation. To be effective and long-lasting - to get the lesson across for life - punishment has to be fair. It will be fair if it's rational, and it's rational if thought out carefully beforehand, as mentioned above. Sometimes, in fact, you can even ask your son or daughter to propose a suggestion of their own for reasonable punishment: "What do you think is fair? Make me an offer." More often than not, surprisingly, their proposals turn out to be reasonable, and sometimes more severe than what you had in mind.

Right to a second chance

This means that, once apologies and restitution are forthcoming, the children start with a clean slate. Children, like all the rest of us, resent grudge-bearing and long memories for past misdeeds that were supposedly forgiven and over with. We do not really forgive unless we also forget. When you truly forgive and forget, you show the children that you disapprove of their faults, not them personally.

Forgiveness like this is crucial, absolutely indispensable for family solidarity. The family is one place in the world where we can always count on a fresh start.

Being just

From time to time, through anger or oversight, you may blunder in doing justice to your children. Nobody's perfect. Whenever this happens, follow up with an apology. If you imposed an excessive punishment, then retract it and scale back to whatever seems reasonable. Don't ever be afraid to say "I'm sorry" to your children, and to explain why. Never fear that you'll seem inconsistent in their eyes. You really are being consistent in what matters most - your heartfelt determination to treat them fairly. When you apologise, you teach them a valuable lesson: you put justice ahead of your ego.

Adults-in-the-making

What are we talking about here? In all of this we're really talking about the way responsible grown-ups try to treat each other. You, like anyone else, would expect other adults to respect your rights to privacy, presumption of innocence, personal dignity, just punishment and so on. You'd expect this treatment from your spouse, your employers, the law. So, *what you're really teaching your children is ethical conduct among responsible adults.* You are treating your children as adults-in-the-making, and you begin by respecting them as people.

Between husband and wife

I used to ask 'veteran parents' (people whose children had grown and flown the nest) what warnings or other negative 'know-how' they'd pass on to younger parents. In paraphrase, here is some of the hard-earned wisdom they shared with me:

To husbands

Don't neglect your wife. She needs what we all need: understanding, affection, gratitude, support and appreciation. For sure, she doesn't get these from the children when they're small. So if she doesn't get them from her husband either, then she doesn't get them at all.

You can tell you're neglecting her if she starts complaining about small things around the house, one after another, circling around the central problem: your apparent unconcern for her. Wake up. Pay attention. Listen to her opinion, help her out, tell her she's great, hug and kiss her from time to time - all this goes a long way. Every time you kiss your wife in front of the children, you are, in effect, kissing each of them in turn.

To wives

Don't undercut your husband. Do all you can to lead your children to respect their father and his authority. He simply cannot lead as a father without his children's abiding respect. Your children's growth in character, their lifelong happiness, can rise or fall on how deeply they respect their dad. So lead them, by your example and your praise for him, to view their father as you do: a great man, a model of masculine strength and accomplishment, a self-sacrificing hero worthy of the whole family's gratitude and honour. Your children's respect for their dad develops directly from your own esteem for him, and this is crucially important to his influence on their lives.

Listen to this story from a man in midwest America: "I was the youngest of five children in a single-parent home. My dad died when I was an infant, so I never knew him. My mother raised us as a widow and she was a great woman. Every now and then, when I was getting out of hand as a boy, and even as a teenager, my mom would take me aside and say, "Jimmy, your father would *never approve* of what you're doing right now! He would be very upset. So stop it..." This never failed to touch me, not once. It always brought me to my senses and made me straighten out."

Do you see? The father of this home continued to influence his children for good, even after his death, because of his great wife's love and honour for him. Because he was still alive in her heart, he was still the father of this family.

To both

Come down to your children's level, but don't stay there. Children are children, and you have to come down to their level to take them by the hand. But your long-term goal is to bring them up to your own level - to lead them, patiently over time, to think and act like mature grown-ups. So live like a grown-up. Enjoy being an adult on top of life, and let them see what this means. If they see you enjoy living as a confident, productive adult, they'll have a life to look forward to.

Finally, don't underestimate your children. Have high ambitions for their swift, step-by-step growth into maturity. We all tend to become what we think about, and children tend to become what their parents expect of them. Even when they sometimes let you down and you have to correct them, make them understand that you see this as just a blip along the way. You have no doubt, none whatever, that they'll someday grow into excellent men and women. You're proud of them, confident in them, and always will be.

Parents and their Adolescent Children

The adventure starts at childhood

The real job of parenthood is to lead children - by example, directed practice, and explanation - so that they grow up to be competent, responsible, considerate men and women who are committed to live by Christian principles all their lives. Your responsibility, in other words, is your children's earthly and eternal happiness - to save their souls from the 'second death' and lead them to the 100-fold in this life that Christ has promised to those who love him.

The way to do this is to form virtues (character strengths) in them - including faith, hope, charity, judgement and conscience, a sense of responsibility, courageous perseverance and self-control. They should live this way before they're out of their teens.

Never forget, the whole of moral development is to move from *self* to *others*. Your children will not grow up when they can take care of themselves, but rather when they can *take care of others* - and want to. The life-outlook of small children is 'Me first!' and the teen years are the time for this attitude to be cast off.

Here are some key ideas to keep in mind - all based on other parents' experience - in leading your adolescent children toward responsible adulthood.

Teach by example

When children deeply respect their parents (by witnessing them live virtuous lives), they remain relatively immune from peer pressures and the sex, drugs and rock 'n' roll culture. If teens do not see their parents as strong, confident leaders, then they pattern their lives after peers and celebrities of the entertainment industry.

See materialism as your family's enemy: the belief that man is just a beast, seeing life end with death, living as though pleasure and power were the purposes of life, treating other human beings as objects.

Communicate and share

Don't underestimate how much you have learned - how much experience and wisdom you can teach them. Share with them.

Start with these questions: What do I know now that I did not know at age 16, and wish I did? Based on my own experience (both successes and mistakes) and what I've seen in others' lives, what can I teach my teens about responsible adult life - making the most of school, finding what you're good at and planning a career, finding or changing a job, dating and courtship, being a loving and supportive husband and wife, social graces, dealing with friends, discerning others, staying in shape, overcoming worries, turning out excellent work, professionalism and professional etiquette, setting priorities and managing time, planning and meeting goals, managing finances, shopping intelligently, knowing nonsense when you see it, staying informed about public affairs, living as a responsible and engaged citizen.

Treat them like adults...

Try to treat your adolescents as what they really are: young adults with everything but experience - which you must now exert yourself to provide. Consider adolescence as the final stage of apprenticeship in growing up, the first stage of real adulthood. Do not treat them as large children. Remember that young people tend to come up or down to our expectations.

Make clear that you want and expect personal best effort, not just results: that they try their best in studies and try to comply with reasonable house rules. Make the rules in your house start with the word "We...." Not, "You must be in by 11:30," but rather, "We all get in at a decent hour." Not, "You must clean up your room," but rather, "We all pitch in to make this house clean and pleasant." Not, "You must apologise," but rather, "We all apologise when we've offended anyone." Give them credit for trying. Be patient.

...but remember they're teenagers!

Bear in mind the powerful influence of body chemistry on their emotions and judgement. They are often uncertain, impulsive, overly sensitive, especially at ages 13 to 17. In many ways, the mood swings of adolescence are like those that children display at ages 2 to 5, and are largely caused by the same growth spurts and hormonal currents within them. So they need the same things they needed from you in their earliest years. They need you to be certain, confidently directive, patient, affectionate, understanding and fair. They also need nutritious food and plenty of sleep.

Don't tell your teens that the high-school years are the best part of their lives. This isn't true. Adolescence, in fact, is one of life's toughest times: coping with blunders and glandular upheavals, surfing up and down learning curves. Tell your children, and above all show them, that every stage of life is interesting, challenging, enjoyable for anyone with a sporting, adventurous spirit. Teens who've been well brought up have a great life ahead of them - like the life they see in you.

Trust them

Distinguish between trusting their *integrity* and trusting their *judgement*. When they ask why you don't trust them, make this clear to them: We implicitly trust your integrity - always have and always will. Unless we have rock-solid evidence otherwise, we trust your honesty and good intentions. What we must sometimes mistrust is your judgement. It's your inexperienced judgement that can make trouble for you and others; when teens get into trouble, the fault is nearly always bad judgement. Be patient. As you gain experience - directly through living, and indirectly through our experienced advice - you will have much stronger judgement, and then we can trust you entirely, right across the board.

Knowing how to correct with love

Remember that 'no' is also a loving word. There's such a thing as loving denial. If young people do not experience their parents' loving denial, then they cannot form the strength of self-denial - and this could lead to tragedy. So, permit nothing in your children's lives that you morally disapprove of. Keep the electronic media under your discerning control. Allow nothing in your home that offends God, undermines your lessons of right and wrong, and treats other people as mere objects. This means no pornography, no gratuitous violence, no glamorous portrayals of sin and disrespect for others. Teach discernment in use of the media: to accept what is good, reject what is wrong - and know the difference.

When you must correct your teens, try to adhere to the same standards you live by when dealing with other adults:

- No public rebukes; whenever possible, correct privately.

- No snap judgements; listen to their side of things. Respect their right to presumption of innocence.

- Don't rub it in. Never say, "I told you so," or "If only you'd listened to me...."

- If emotions are getting out of control, put off discussion till later: "Let's talk about this tomorrow night." (Waiting is itself a sort of punishment.)

If you've overreacted, apologise. They will respect your desire to be fair: you try to put justice and truth ahead of your pride.

In worst-case scenarios, you may rely on restrictions on use of the telephone, restrictions on driver's license and use of car, or use of computers and the internet.

Don't get trapped into blazing arguments and most especially if you have a temper. Words can wound and take a long time to heal. Again, if tempers are flaring, put off the discussion till later - that evening or the next day - when you've both cooled down. If you go too far, be the first to apologise.

Awareness of their everyday lives

Be aware that the present-day materialistic teen culture is bogus and unrealistic - a fairly new movement that turns adolescents into an artificial leisure class, similar in lifestyle to that of previous ages' corrupt aristocrats: abundant leisure time, irresponsible avoidance of work, hedonistic abuse of food and alcohol, unlimited access to drugs and recreational sex, life centred around play, flight from boredom, fear only for sexually transmitted disease. The teen culture is itself countercultural.

Real life - which is what you're trying to teach - consists of loving sacrifice, responsible commitments, productive and service-oriented work, affectionate relationships with family and friends, enjoyment of food, drink and leisure pursuits in healthy moderation, being loved and respected by all who know us.

Markers for progress

How can you tell that you are making progress with your children, that they are really growing up, especially in their early teens? In several ways:

Generally speaking, they are aware of the rights and feelings of others, and act this way; they have a habit of work, putting their powers up against problems; in family life, they are conscious of being needed (that is, they know the meaning of *responsibility*: if we don't do our duty, someone else will suffer); they live like producers, not consumers; they can take care of others, and want to; most of the time, in a host of situations, they do the right thing without being told; when they've done wrong, they know it and apologises; also, they accept readily the apologies of others, and they forget as well as forgive; they say, and mean, *please* and *thank you* and *I'm sorry*; they keep their promises. They will endure hardship rather than break their word; most of their blunders come not from ill will or selfishness, but rather from lack of experience; by and large, they try to do the right thing; deep down, they know their parents' corrections come from love: they sense that their parents correct them *because* they love them; they refrain from whatever would disgrace their family; they choose friends of upright character; their prayers are addressed to God as a *person* - so they see sin as a rupture of their personal friendship with God, an offence calling for apology and amendment. They see the Church as an extension of their family - worthy of their love and loyalty, no matter what; people outside the family - friends and neighbours - compliment the parents for their children's character.

Looking forward

Remember that your children may forget most of the details of what you teach them, but they will remember what was *important* to you. For most of us, the lifelong voice of conscience is the voice of our parents - God speaking to us through the memory of what our parents lovingly taught us.

When your children leave home for college, tell them: "Do not forget that God is watching over you with love, as he has since your childhood. Do not offend him, and do nothing that would betray what you learned in our family. We will pray for you every day. Remember that God commands all of us, 'Honour your father and mother.' And the way we honour our parents is this: we adopt their values as our own, live by them all our lives, and then pass them on to our own children whole and intact."

Family Health-Check

Children in trouble

Something is seriously wrong in today's society. For some reasons, large numbers of parents around us are failing to form character in their children. We look around in our workplaces and neighbourhoods and see young people in their twenties who are immature and irresolute, soft and irresponsible, uneasy about themselves and their futures. They may be technically skilled in some field and hold down decently paying jobs, but their personal lives and marriages are unstable. In their conduct and attitudes, these young people seem permanently stuck in adolescence, that dangerous mixture of adult powers and childlike irresponsibility. Some are crippled or destroyed by substance abuse.

But even if they remain drug-free (what a strange term!), many see their professional work as mere ego gratification or (an adolescent attitude) just drudgery endured for the sake of earning and spending money. Great numbers of them live as heartless or indifferent narcissists, caring little or nothing about their parents or children, if they choose to have any. They retain within themselves, sometimes tragically, the flawed attitudes and habits of childhood. For some reason, they never quite grew up.

It's clear, certainly, that many young people like this were wounded by a childhood spent in dysfunctional families: drug and alcohol dependency, physical and sexual abuse, hopeless poverty. But what is striking today, and more to our point here, is the huge percentage of seriously troubled youths from so-called 'normal' families. It seems that in our society the distinction between normal and dysfunctional has blurred. Or, to put it another way, some sort of subtle dysfunction is corroding large numbers of typical, middle-class homes.

We see the results of this all around us. Children today grow up in busy families where father and mother live together, life is comfortable and physically secure, and yet the children grow up troubled. What is going wrong in our supposedly normal middle-class families today that could account for these problems? What is happening - or not happening - at home such that children grow older without growing up, that they arrive at adulthood without enough judgement and will and conscience to set their lives straight?

Let's approach the problem this way:

Normal families seem to fall into two broad categories. One we could call the self-absorbed *consumerist* family; the second the character-forming *sporting adventure* family.

In the self-absorbed family, parents do not set out, on purpose, to form character in their children. They treat family life like a picnic, a passive pleasure-centered experience, and their children often meet with later trouble.

In the *sporting adventure* family, by contrast, parents do set out to form character, and they work at this for years. As a result, their family life becomes an ideal-driven adventure, a great sport, and their children largely turn out well. Why is this?

Let's look at the self-absorbed family.

Consumerist parents are self-absorbed and unconcerned with growth in character strengths (that is, virtues), whether for themselves or their children. So they make family life mostly a steady series of pleasant diversions. Life for parents and children centres around leisurely enjoyment, fun-filled entertainment - a seamless array of sports, abundant food and drink, television shows, computer games, movies, music, parties, shopping.

Boredom, it seems, is the consumerist family's enemy, to be shunned at all costs. So children in families like this are kept relentlessly busy, constantly amused. The parents' rules in the house, if any, aim mainly at damage control: keeping squabbles and hassles to a minimum, keeping the children out of trouble, keeping the children from wrecking the place.

Consequently, in consumerist homes children are steadily apprenticed through childhood as consumers, not producers. Every day, they avidly practice living as self-absorbed enjoyers and shoppers. Not surprisingly, youngsters from such picnic-like homes see life as mostly play, a lifetime entitlement to happy amusement. The life of grown-up work (as they dimly understand it) is solely for piling up spending money - working in order to spend, producing only in order to consume. Who can blame them for this life-outlook? After all, this is all they experience in family life; and, as we've seen, children learn character mostly from personal example and repeated experience.

Sooner or later, of course, endless fun dwindles into boredom; people start seeking other alluring diversions. And the same happens in the picnic-like consumerist family. Starting in their middle-school years, an appalling number of self-absorbed children grow bored with juvenile amusements and avidly turn to novel kinds of powerfully pleasurable sensations, including alcohol and other drugs. Children raised to see life as play will treat the automobile as a toy, and so will be prone to be reckless. Because their life has centered on things, they're disposed to put things ahead of people - to treat people as objects, mere tools and toys for their use or amusement. Related to this, they see sex as a toy, a high-powered form of recreation, and so fall headlong into promiscuity, co-habitational relations, unwanted pregnancies, abortions and disastrous marriages. This is no exaggeration. It happens literally every day.

Symptoms: parents

- Consumerist parents live divided lives. They live as producers at work, but consumers at home. In fact, to their children they seem to work only in order to consume. Their home, far removed as it is from the real-life world of responsible adult achievement and ethical interpersonal dealings, is a place arrayed with entertainment gadgets, a site devoted to comfort, relaxation and amusement. But this universe of comfortable delight is all that their children see - and for children, 'seeing is believing.' This cocoon of pleasant escapism wholly envelopes children and shapes their sole experience with life. It becomes the ambiance within which they fashion their deepest attitudes and habits, indeed their whole outlook on life: 'Life is all about pleasure.'

- Being self-absorbed and centred mainly on the present, consumerist parents seldom think about their children's futures - that is, what sort of men and women their children will grow up to become. Their time horizon stretches, at most, only a few months or couple of years ahead. Almost never do they picture their children as grown men and women in their late twenties with job and family responsibilities of their own. When the parents do think of their childrens' futures, they think in terms of career, not character. They think of what their children will *do*, not who they will *be*.

- The parents seem to expect - in fact, utterly take for granted - that their children will naturally grow up okay as long as they're kept busily amused and shielded (more or less) from outside influences. In other words, they think that adult-level ethics, conscience and sound judgement will form in their children in a natural and unaided way, along with the children's physical stature. When the parents think of character at all, they think it's something to be *maintained* in children, rather than encouraged and developed.

- The parents come down to the children's level, as indeed all parents should - but (and here's the point) they *stay* there. By their own evident devotion to a 'hassle-free' existence at home, off the job, they neglect to raise their children to grown-up levels of responsible thinking and acting. They do little to prepare the children for later life and lead them toward responsible service. Indeed, their children seem to have no concept what adulthood means - except for what they see in movies and television dramas. The parents seem clueless that they have a job to do, an action to take, a change to make in their children's minds, hearts, and wills: to strengthen each child's conscience and character for life.

- Both parents give in readily to children's wishes and feelings, even when they judge that this might be a mistake. Often in family life they permit what they disapprove of. That is, they let children's pleas and whining override their parental misgivings. The parents are moved by their children's smiles, not their welfare, and so they will give in on many issues to avoid a scene. Unwittingly, through their example of giving in, these parents teach their children to let strong desires or whims routinely override judgements of conscience. So the children fail to distinguish between wants and needs; to the children, wants *are* needs. As a result, feelings, not conscience, become a guide for action. (So, what happens later when the children are tempted by the powerfully pleasurable sensations of drugs, alcohol, promiscuous sex? What is there to hold them back?)

- The father is a weak moral figure in the home. He does not teach right from wrong in a confident, purposeful way, and does nothing to prepare his older children for their later lives outside the home, especially in moral matters. He defers 'children's things' to his wife. To his children, he appears mostly as an amiable, somewhat dull figure, even a sort of older sibling. In family life, the children see him wrapped up entirely in his own leisure activities (like watching television, playing sports) and minor repairs. Since they never see him work, they have no idea how he earns his living or even what this term means. Moreover, he seldom shows much outward respect and gratitude toward his wife - so she, too, seems a weak figure to the children.

- Parents are minimal in practising religion. Though the family may attend a house of worship from time to time, even regularly, this is done as thoughtless social routine. Family life includes little or no prayer, neither before meals nor at any other time. So children never witness their parents living a sense of responsibility toward God or some strong internalised ethic. 'God' is just a word (sometimes an expletive), not a person, certainly not a friend. In the children's eyes, parents do not seem answerable to anyone or anything, except a relentlessly busy calendar.

- Parents watch television indiscriminately and allow adult entertainment into the home. Though they may restrict, more or less, their children's access to inappropriate material, they are driving home a powerful message: 'When you're old enough, anything goes.' Consequently, to the children, the right-wrong dichotomy becomes strictly a matter of age: 'Whatever's wrong for children is okay for grown-ups, so just wait till I turn 16!'

Symptoms: children

- At first glance most children from consumerist homes don't seem seriously troubled at all. Typically they're cheery and well scrubbed, pleasant and smiling, often very active - but only for things they enjoy. They're habituated to pleasant sensations. They like to be liked, and in fact they expect to be liked no matter what they do. Since they're used to treating adults (including their parents) as equals, they appear naïvely lacking in respectful good manners. With some troubled exceptions here and there, they seem entirely carefree. Indeed most of them really are carefree, for now.

- Children have a low tolerance for discomfort or even inconvenience. They are horrified by physical pain, however slight, or even the threat of it. They successfully plead, badger and stall their way out of unpleasant commitments - promises and previous agreements, music lessons, homework, chores, appointments, deadlines.

- Children believe that just about anything may be done for a laugh. If a prank or ridiculing remark toward someone amuses them and their peers, they blithely indulge in it no matter who gets hurt. They think their entitlement to fun overrides other people's rights and feelings. Indeed, the existence of other people's rights and feelings almost never enters their minds. Their outlook on life remains unchanged from infancy: 'Me first!'

- Children enjoy an abundance of spending money and leisure time. As a fixed habit, they overindulge in soft drinks, sweets and junk food. They spend countless hours wholly absorbed in electronic sensations (computer games, television, the internet) and other types of amusement. They are generally free to consume whatever they want whenever they want it, and so they do.

- Children show little or no respect for people outside the family: guests, their parents' friends, teachers, the elderly. They seldom, if ever, display good manners in public. *Please* and *thank you* are missing from their speech. On birthdays or holidays, children rip through a mound of presents, but neglect to write or call to say thank you - and see no reason to. In some instances, children may be superficially pleasant to people (as long as this costs them nothing) but have zero concern for others' needs or interests.

- Ironically, for all the parents' efforts to provide a pleasant home, the children hold little or no respect for them. The children view their parents as 'nice,' and they'll admit they 'like' Mum and Dad most of the time. But they simply do not esteem their parents as strong, and therefore emulable, people. When asked whom they do admire, they rattle off a list of entertainment figures.

- Children know next to nothing about their parents' personal histories, and nothing at all about grandparents and forebears. So they have no sense of family history and moral continuity, that is, how they are the latest in a long line of mutually loving people who struggled, often heroically, to serve each other and stick together through good times and bad.

- The children have no heroes in their lives, no real people or historical or literary figures who surpassed themselves in service to others and, by fulfilling duties, accomplished great deeds. In the absence of heroes to imitate, the children admire and pattern themselves after coarsely freakish media celebrities. (As someone wise once said, 'If children have no heroes, they'll follow after clowns.')

- Children don't care about causing embarrassment to the family. Often they don't even understand what that might mean, for they have no framework for grasping what is shameful. They are unmoved by any cultivated sense of 'family honour'. If children's dress and public behaviour cause shame to the parents, that's just too bad.

- Children complain and whine about situations that can't be helped: bad weather, reasonable delays, physical discomfort, moderately heavy workloads, personality differences and the like. Their most common word of complaint is 'boring.' Since their lives at home are micromanaged rather than directed, they're accustomed to having their problems solved by oversolicitous grown-ups. They've found through experience that if they hold out long enough, someone will eventually step in to make their troubles go away. Consequently, they learn to escape problems, not solve them. They learn to shun rather than endure discomfort.

- Children have no serious hobbies except watching television, playing computer games, surfing the internet and listening to music. Their lives seem entirely plugged in to electronic devices and they don't know what to do without them. Their thinking is dominated by the entertainment culture; in some senses, they *believe* in it. They know the words to songs and commercials, but know nothing of the Ten Commandments.

- Children (even older ones and teens) tend to form opinions by impulse and vague impressions. They are scarcely ever pressed to rely on reasons and factual evidence for their judgements. Thus they're easily swayed by flattery, emotional appeals and peer-group pressures. They fail to recognise claptrap - as in advertising, pop culture and politics - when they see it. They follow the crowd wherever it goes.

- Children never ask the question 'Why?' except to defy directions from rightful authority. They are intellectually dull, even inert, showing little curiosity about life outside their family-school-playground universe. In school, moreover, they are careless in work and do not take correction seriously. For them, nearly all enjoyment comes from escapist amusement, not from work well done, serious accomplishment, fulfilment of duty, serving others or personal goals achieved through purposeful effort. If a task isn't 'fun' they're not interested.

- Children have little sense of time. Since they hardly ever have to wait for something they want, much less earn it, they have unrealistic expectations about the time needed to complete a task. They estimate either too much or too little. Consequently, large tasks are put off too long or small jobs appear mountainous. Even older children approaching secondary school age have virtually no concept of deadline or of working steadily within a self-imposed time frame. The children seem to drift along in a free-floating, ever-present *now* - and this state of mind continues well into adolescence and even young adulthood.

• Throughout secondary school and college, school is viewed as one last fling at life, not a preparation for it. Graduation looms as a poignantly sad event, for they see the best part of life as behind them, not ahead. What lies ahead is trouble - the 'hassles' (as they put it) of real-life work, responsible commitments, day-to-day routine, budgets and bills, two-week holidays and diminished freedom. So who looks forward to this? Who can endure it? Why grow up?

This picture of a family headed for trouble is just a composite sketch, not a comprehensive description. Certainly there are gradations among families; some families will show some of these characteristics, but not all of them. Nonetheless, over and over again, the features listed here show up in the personal histories of troubled adolescents and young adults who have come - we must stress this again - from apparently healthy homes.

Effective Parenting in a Nutshell

The real threat of materialism is not the pursuit of things. It is, rather, seeing and treating other people as things - and therefore putting things ahead of people. Youngsters with a habit of thinking and acting this way are headed toward trouble later in life. So what can parents do with their young children now to build strong character and lead children away from materialism?

Have confidence

Be confident of your rightful authority as a parent and insist that your children respect it. Your responsibility as a parent is enormous, and you must exercise a self-confident, loving authority to carry it out. Your children's confidence in your leadership will derive from your own self-confident sense of mission.

Cultivate character and virtue

Remember that you're raising adults, not children. When you think of your children's future, picture character as well as career. Your job is not to keep children amused and busy. It is, rather, to lead your children to become competent, responsible, considerate and generous men and women who are committed to live by principles of integrity. Think of who your children will *be*, not just what they will *do*.

Teach the great character strengths (virtues): prudence, justice, fortitude, temperance and charity. In today's terms, these are called sound judgement and conscience, a sense of responsibility, courageous perseverance, self-mastery, and respect for the rights and sensibilities of others. You teach these strengths in three ways: by your personal example, your direction of your children's behaviour, and your verbal explanations of right and wrong. But you teach mostly by example. Remember that conscience is the memory of our parents' voices, their loving lessons of right and wrong taught to us in our youth.

Teach courtesy

Teach your children the four great pillars of civilised dealings with others: 'please,' 'thank you,' 'I'm sorry' and 'I give my word'. Using these habitually in speech is a basis for respecting the rights of others.

Teach the value of service

Raise your children to be producers, not consumers. Let them put their powers up against problems to solve them, and thus grow into healthy self-confidence. Lead them to take schoolwork and chores seriously so they will learn the meaning of responsible service. We were born to love and serve one another, not to shop. Children do not grow up when they can take care of themselves; they really grow up when they can take care of *others* - and want to.

Teach patience

Make your children wait for something they want, and if possible make them earn it. Waiting and earning are part of responsible adult life, which is what you are after. Let the children learn the difference between wants and needs. Let them see that 'everyone else else has one' and 'everyone else is doing it' are, at best, lame reasons for any course of action. Sound judgement and conscience are guides for life, and should never give way to thoughtless conformity.

Teach integrity

Teach your children the meaning of the word 'integrity.' Integrity means unity of intention, word and action - that is, we mean what we say, we say what we mean, and we keep our word. We always tell the truth and we keep our promises.

Don't let your children weasel out of commitments. Don't let them take back their word on a whim. Before they make promises or otherwise commit themselves to a course of action, press them to think the consequences through and understand their terms, because you will hold them to their word. If they want to buy a pet, make them first commit themselves to feeding and caring for it - then hold them to that. If they accept an invitation (after first checking with you), they're obliged to attend even if something more alluring turns up.

Learn to say 'no' to help them

Realise that 'no' is also a loving word, and your children must hear it from time to time in order to acquire self-control.

Children who never experience loving parental denial cannot form the concept of self-denial - and this can later lead to disaster. Practice 'affectionate assertiveness' in disciplining your children. Correct the fault, not the person; hate the sin, love the sinner. Show your children you love them too much to let them grow up with their faults uncorrected.

Keep an eye on the media

Keep the electronic media under your discerning control. Permit nothing in your home that undermines your lessons of right and wrong and treats other people as mere things. Teach discernment in use of the media: to accept what is good, reject what is wrong, and know the difference.

Listen!

Listen to your children. Learn what is going on in their developing minds and guide them with your responsible judgement. Live as a responsible adult who's on top of life, and let them learn what this means.

Never forget: You have one chance - and only one - to raise your children right. Forming your children's character and conscience is your number one priority. If you make a sacrificial effort now, while your children are still young, you can later enjoy the honour they bring you as confident, responsible, considerate men and women - who strive to pass on your values to their own children in turn.

Reading list

More titles from the author, published by Scepter:

Compass: A Handbook on Parent Leadership
(ISBN 1-59417-000-2)

Lifeline: The Religious Upbringing of Your Children
(ISBN 0-933932-97-9)

Father, the Family Protector
(ISBN 1-59417-033-9)

www.parentleadership.com